Federal Land Transfers

The Conservation Foundation is a nonprofit research and communications organization dedicated to encouraging human conduct to sustain and enrich life on earth. Since its founding in 1948, it has attempted to provide intellectual leadership in the cause of wise management of the earth's resources.

Federal Land Transfers:
The Case for a Westwide Program Based on the Federal Land Policy and Management Act

by Frank Gregg

The Conservation Foundation
Washington, D.C.

Federal Land Transfers: The Case for a Westwide Program Based on the Federal Land Policy and Management Act

Cover design by Sally A. Janin

Typeset by VIP Systems, Inc., Alexandria, Virginia

Printed by Edwards Brothers, Inc., Ann Arbor, Michigan

The Conservation Foundation
1717 Massachusetts Avenue, N.W.
Washington, DC 20036

Library of Congress Cataloging in Publication Data
Gregg, Frank, 1925-
    Federal land transfers.

    (An Issue Report)
    Includes bibliographical references.
    1. West (U.S.)—Public lands—Management.
    2. United States—Public lands—Management.
I. Title. II. Series: Issue report (Conservation Foundation)
HD243.A17G73 1982   333.1'6'0978   82-8126
ISBN 0-89164-071-1

CONTENTS

Foreword

Several proposals have been made recently to trade or sell large amounts of public lands—particularly those, concentrated in the West, managed by the Bureau of Land Management (BLM). The state of Utah proposed in 1981 a huge package of exchanges and other transfers to block up state lands. This year, proposals emerging from the White House and Congress call for selling millions of acres of public lands to help balance the federal budget. As Frank Gregg writes in this paper, "Literally tens of millions of acres of land and billions of dollars in resource values would change hands if 'blocking up' were pursued seriously in the West." An aggressive program to sell federal lands could have similarly far-reaching results.

Clearly, the landownership patterns in many areas of the West are nothing short of chaotic. Often, state and private lands are intermingled, in the classic checkerboard pattern, with federal lands managed by BLM. In other cases, where federal holdings are fairly well consolidated, state and private lands exist as isolated parcels in their midst; or the reverse situation may prevail, with federal lands isolated and inaccessible. In both cases, the minority owner's use of land is influenced—and often inhibited—by the majority landowner's activity or inactivity. Given the expense of management of scattered and isolated parcels, and the fact that some economically valuable lands, as well as lands of recreational, wilderness, and scientific potential, are unusable or inaccessible in their present state, an expeditious but deliberate exchange program would seem to be in everyone's best interest, so long as no party profits at the expense of others. As Gregg writes in this paper, "At stake are not just acres. Rather, the larger issue is the potential effect on the value and manageability of public lands and related private, state, and other federal lands when transfers are not preceded by careful and open deliberations on desirable ownership patterns, values, and uses."

Gregg contends that exchanges and sale offerings can be consummated without undue delay, and with full public discussion of the issues involved, within the context of the Federal Land Policy and Management Act (FLPMA). The Utah proposal and other exchange and sale proposals are important not only in themselves, but as symptoms of a larger problem—the quest for instant solutions to complex, long-standing problems. There is a grave danger that the search for simple "quick fixes" that undermine established planning processes will invite suspicion, stridency, and stalemate.

Frank Gregg served as Director of the Bureau of Land Management, Department of the Interior, from 1978 to 1981. He began this paper while he was on The Conservation Foundation staff for several months in 1981, consulting on our Land Program. He completed it while in his present position as a visiting professor with the School of Renewable Natural Resources, University of Arizona, Tucson. We believe that the issues the report raises, and the procedures for effecting transfers under FLPMA that Gregg describes and analyzes, should be discussed widely, not just by the federal and state officials immediately involved, but by all those concerned about the future of those federal lands prized by so many people for so many uses. All Americans have an important stake in the future use and possible disposition of our public lands. Policies for these lands are now being reconsidered and significant new directions are evident. This paper is intended to inform and sharpen the current debate.

The Conservation Foundation is deeply grateful to the Richard King Mellon Foundation, the American Conservation Association, and an anonymous donor for assistance to our public land research.

William K. Reilly
President
The Conservation Foundation

Acknowledgments

I am grateful to Christopher J. Duerksen, Robert G. Healy, Michael Mantell, John H. Noble, and William E. Shands of the Foundation staff, who helped with both the format and substance of the report. The Foundation's librarian, Barbara K. Rodes, provided spirited assistance, ferreting out a number of scarce reference materials, public land data, and current legislation on land transfers.

Frank Gregg

Executive Summary

The 174 million acres of public lands managed by the Department of the Interior's Bureau of Land Management in 11 western states (excluding Alaska)—the lands remaining of the public domain—are distributed across the West in random patterns, ranging from relatively solid blocks to small, isolated tracts interspersed among lands in state and private ownership. The existing configuration of intermingled public and private landownership creates for the various owners problems of administrative efficiency and effective economic use for resource-based activities. The pattern also inhibits management of natural systems fragmented by multiple ownerships. Large-scale exchanges and other forms of land transfers offer the opportunity to improve the efficiency and effectiveness of management of federal, state, and private lands in the West.

This paper argues that the most promising mechanism for effecting these transfers to achieve optimum economic and environmental values for all the interests involved is through the Federal Land Policy and Managment Act (FLPMA), enacted by Congress in 1976 as the "organic act" for the public lands. FLPMA established the policy of retaining the remaining public lands, while also authorizing their exchange and disposal guided by "public interest" and "national interest" tests and by "equal value" and "fair market value" concepts. Using these policies as general guidelines, this paper recommends that decisions about public land retention and transfers be addressed throughout the West through an accelerated land-use planning process under FLPMA, with extensive public participation.

Now before Congress are several bills for major transfers of public lands that would bypass the provisions of FLPMA. Also outside the guidelines of FLPMA are current Administration proposals to use public lands as "currency" to acquire lands for national parks, forests, monuments, seashores, and wild and scenic rivers; and to sell public lands to bolster the treasury. A major land-transfer effort under consideration that does not involve the land-use planning and public involvement provided for in FLPMA is Utah Governor Matheson's "Project Bold" proposal for a massive direct exchange of lands between the state of Utah and the Department of the Interior. These and other proposals to "end run" FLPMA assume that the act's required planning processes are obstacles to efficient land transfers, involving complexity, excessive costs, and time. But attempts to bypass FLPMA, while appearing to promise short cuts in time and procedure, will inevitably generate fears and allegations of "giveaway," as *ad hoc* and isolated decisions and deals are made, creating an atmosphere that ultimately thwarts desirable transfers.

As an alternative to bypassing FLPMA, this paper proposes a two-year federal initiative to make FLPMA work. The Secretary of the Interior, in unusually careful consultation with the Congress and the governors (including those outside the West), could provide a sense of purpose for land transfers in the form of a deliberate program operating within the policies and processes set forth in FLPMA. The program would identify those lands that should remain in federal multiple-use management, evaluate and facilitate large-scale exchanges where ownership patterns suggest the need, and identify those public lands that might best be offered for disposal, either as trading stock for consolidation of existing federal areas or through outright disposal.

This proposed process, involving formal cooperation with governors, state land commissions, and the public is, in effect, a revision and updating of the previous classification of public lands for retention and disposal under the Classification and Multiple Use Act of 1964, modified to include large-scale exchanges and using FLPMA authorities, mandates, and processes. The two-year planning period of land classification would be followed by aggressive implementation of exchange and disposal decisions.

Given the controversy surrounding public lands management, it is essential to gain and sustain public confidence for a large-scale program of land transfers. Conducted under an existing law, following explicit and generally accepted procedures, the program proposed in this paper would be perceived as more equitable than would a series of *ad hoc* proposals subject to characterization as deals and open to political attack and judicial challenge.

Who should—or can—take the lead in championing a rational approach to landownership patterns in the West? Because of its prior commitments to transfers outside the FLPMA framework, and credibility problems with environmental and other interests, Administration initiatives may be both unlikely and not universally welcome. The national and public interest would be well served if Utah's highly respected Governor Matheson should propose that his Project Bold—the first comprehensive statewide effort to rationalize state and public land patterns—be concluded under FLPMA, setting a precedent which offers a genuine prospect of replication in the other western states. Congress should, in any event, exercise its oversight responsibilities through hearings to assess the consistency of current Administration policies and actions relating to land transfers with law, legislative intent, and various perspectives of the public interest.

Introduction

THE PUBLIC LANDS

The public lands* managed by the Bureau of Land Management (BLM)—174 million acres in 11 western states (see Table 1) and additional millions of acres in Alaska—are, literally, the remnants of the public domain. These lands have remained in federal ownership after disposal of hundreds of millions of other acres of the public domain—to states for the support of public schools and other purposes; to private companies as inducements to build the transcontinental railroads; to individuals as homesteads and veterans' bonuses; to other federal agencies as units of the national park, forest, and wildlife refuge systems; and to other recipients for numerous other purposes. The remaining estate includes much of the nation's mineral wealth; rangelands that sustain a vigorous livestock industry and provide key habitats for wildlife; critical watershed areas; and areas of extraordinary scenic, wilderness, recreational, and archaeological values.

Public lands do not lie in uniformly compact units. Individuals who obtained public lands under various disposal statutes chose those tracts most attractive for their needs. States typically received between two and four specified tracts of 640 acres each from the public domain in every township. Grants to railroads were usually in the form of alternate sections for a stated distance on each side of the right-of-way, which created giant checkerboards up to 60 miles wide and hundreds of miles long.

---

*As used in this paper, *public lands* usually refers to those lands managed by BLM, although national forests, administered by the U.S. Forest Service (U.S. Department of Agriculture), national parks, and wildlife refuges are also publicly owned federal lands.

TABLE 1

LANDS UNDER EXCLUSIVE JURISDICTION OF THE BUREAU OF LAND MANAGEMENT IN 10 WESTERN STATES, 1980[1]

State	Acreage
Arizona	12,566,813
California	16,327,523
Colorado	8,165,544
Idaho	11,941,728
Montana	8,149,791
Nevada	48,747,005
New Mexico	12,769,833
Oregon	15,717,606
Utah	22,074,731
Wyoming	17,794,789

Source: U.S. Department of the Interior, Bureau of Land Management, *Public Land Statistics, 1980* (Washington, D.C.: Government Printing Office, 1981).

[1] The state of Washington is not included in the table because it contains a comparatively small amount of public land acreage—approximately 300,000 acres. Public lands in Alaska have been the subject of special legislation and controversy and are not covered by the proposal outlined in this paper.

The remaining public lands are distributed across the West in a variety of patterns, including relatively solid blocks, federal portions of the checkerboards, and scattered small tracts. Problems of access to isolated tracts, of conflicting management objectives on intermingled lands, of administrative efficiency, and of assembly of economic units for various kinds of resource-based development activities are common.

Large-scale land exchanges between federal and state governments—and, in the railroad checkerboards, between federal, state, and private owners—could benefit the public substantially by "blocking up" holdings in the interest of more efficient administration and more effective use and management of resources. Literally tens of millions of acres of land and billions of dollars in resource values could change hands if "blocking up" were to be pursued seriously in the West. (See Table 2 for state "trust" land acreages, the lands the states would use for trading stock.) Given the often near-random patterns of public, state, and private lands in a rapidly growing and politically restive West, interest in dis-

TABLE 2

APPROXIMATE ACREAGE OF STATE "SCHOOL LANDS" AND OTHER TRUST LANDS STILL HELD BY 10 WESTERN STATES[1]

State	Acreage
Arizona	9,581,976
California	4,000,000
Colorado	3,000,000
Idaho	2,520,065
Montana	5,224,247
Nevada	0
New Mexico	9,222,698
Oregon	765,493
Utah	3,629,122
Wyoming	3,654,878

Source: Figures provided by Rowena Rogers, Chairman, Western Land Commissioners Association.

[1] These are primarily lands acquired by grant from the federal government upon admission to statehood or by special act thereafter which are still held in state ownerships. Over the years, the states have disposed of substantial acreages of grant land: Nevada, for example, has disposed of all the 2.7 million acres granted it by the federal government.

The lands are administered by state land boards or commissions for the purpose of generating revenues for support of schools, universities, and other beneficiaries. Trust lands which have been dedicated to state parks and wildlife areas are not included in these figures. These are the lands which would form the primary basis of a major state-federal exchange program.

posal and exchange of public lands is frequently and forcefully expressed.

The current interest in land transfers offers an opportunity for a serious—perhaps historic—effort to improve the efficiency and effectiveness of management of both federal and state lands (and, to a lesser extent, private lands) in the West to achieve optimum economic and environmental values. The Federal Land Policy and Management Act provides authority, policy guidance, and processes that may be used to support an aggressive public land exchange and judicious disposal program with assured opportunity for participation by all interests, and consideration of the full range of natural resource values. At stake are not just acres. Rather, the larger issue is the potential effect on the value and manageability of public lands and related private, state, and other federal lands when transfers are not preceded by careful and open deliberations on desirable ownership patterns, values, and uses.

THE FEDERAL LAND POLICY AND MANAGEMENT ACT (FLPMA)

In 1976, after years of debate based largely on the 1970 report of the congressionally chartered Public Land Law Review Commission (PLLRC), Congress enacted the Federal Land Policy and Management Act (FLPMA). FLPMA was to serve as an "organic act" for BLM and to guide the management of the public lands over the long term.

FLPMA reversed a long-standing assumption that the public lands were ultimately to be disposed of to other owners and managers:

> The Congress finds and declares that it is the policy of the United States that—
>
> (1) the public lands be retained in federal ownership, unless as a result of the land use planning procedure provided for in this Act, it is determined that disposal of a particular parcel will serve the national interest.

This declaration was consistent with PLLRC's recommendation on disposal.[1]

The general retention policy was clearly qualified, however, for FLPMA also provided procedural tools for land disposal and exchange. First, the act describes in some detail a land-use planning procedure to determine, among other things, the "national interest" in disposal of particular tracts. Then it sets forth detailed rules for exchanges of public land, where these are found to be in the "public interest," and offers guidance on land sales. The following provisions of FLPMA bear most directly on public land exchange and disposal:

• The public lands are to be retained in federal ownership, unless, as a result of the land-use planning process provided for in FLPMA, it is determined that disposal of a particular parcel will serve the national interest. *Sec. 102 (a)(1).*

• The United States is to receive fair market value for use of

public lands and resources unless otherwise provided by law. *Sec. 102 (a)(9)*.

• Uniform procedures are to apply to public land disposal, acquisition, and exchange, with authority reserved to the Congress to review disposals in excess of a specified acreage. *Sec. 102 (2)(10)*.

• BLM, with public involvement, and in coordination with other federal agencies and Indian tribes, is to prepare and maintain land-use plans. *Sec. 202*. Those plans are to be consistent with state and local plans within the limits of federal law. *Sec. 202 (c) (9)*.

• Public lands may be *sold* at a price not less than fair market value when land-use planning determines that a sale would meet certain criteria* relating to manageability, community expansion needs, and other public objectives. *Sec. 203 (a)*. FLPMA also requires congressional review of sales of tracts of over 2,500 acres. *Sec. 203 (c)*.

• Public land or interests may be disposed of by *exchange* where the Secretary of the Interior finds such exchange will serve the public interest. Consideration is to be given to better federal land management and the needs of state and local people, including needs for the economy, community expansion, recreation areas, food, fiber, minerals, and fish and wildlife. The Secretary must find that "the values and the objectives which federal lands or interests to be conveyed may serve if retained in federal ownership are not more than the values of the nonfederal lands or interests and the public objectives that could be served if acquired." All lands involved in a specific exchange must lie within the same state. The values of lands exchanged must be equal, except that values may be equalized by payment of up to 25 percent of total value. *Sec. 206*.

• In the case of all conveyances *except exchanges*, minerals and certain exploration rights are to be reserved to the federal government (with provision for exception). *Sec. 209*.

• The governor and affected local officials must be notified at least 60 days in advance of any conveyance of public land. *Sec. 210*.

• The Secretary shall provide opportunities for public participation, and promulgate regulations establishing public participation procedures. *Sec. 202 (f)*.

---

*The criteria in these sections are *refinements* of the "national interest" test required in Sec. 102(a)(1) for disposal of public lands.

CURRENT PROPOSALS TO BYPASS FLPMA

Despite the long congressional debate on major provisions of FLPMA—including the involvement of key members of Congress in the work of the PLLRC—recent proposals for disposal and other transfers of public land have, in a number of cases, indicated a clear preference for bypassing FLPMA as the basis for analysis and action. A few examples suggest the nature and scale of potential transfers.

Proposals from Washington

The Secretary of the Interior has proposed that public lands be used as the primary "currency" to compensate owners of lands to be acquired for national parks, monuments, seashores, wild and scenic rivers, and national forest wilderness areas. (Acquisition costs would otherwise be drawn from the Land and Water Conservation Fund.) Federal agencies in 1980 estimated (through the Land Policy Group, which convenes the acquiring agencies on issues involving the fund) that costs of then-authorized acquisitions would be considerably over $3 billion. This would mean a potential demand on public land of substantial proportions if all such acquisitions were to be accomplished through exchanges of public land (Table 3).

In February 1982, President Reagan established a Real Property Review Board, composed of White House aides and cabinet officers, to "develop and monitor policies for acquisition, utilization and disposal of Federal real property assets." Public lands will be sold ". . . to provide early opportunities for community expansion and industrial development. . . ." While the Administration said that it plans to dispose primarily of "small, isolated, and unproductive lands,"[2] there is the prospect that lands considered for sales will not be given adequate analysis from the perspective of natural resource values and best appropriate land use.

Pending legislation adds to the picture of diverse and conflicting demands for public lands disposal.

H.R. 1137, introduced by Congressman Manuel Lujan (R-New Mexico) with companion legislation in the Senate, would authorize New Mexico to select about 400,000 acres of public lands in exchange for a like acreage of state lands within the White Sands Missile Range. Congressman Lujan also has proposed (H.R. 2139)

TABLE 3

ESTIMATED COSTS OF PLANNED AND AUTHORIZED FEDERAL LAND ACQUISITIONS ELIGIBLE FOR FUNDING THROUGH LAND AND WATER CONSERVATION FUND (L&WCF)[1]
(in millions)

Agency	Specific[2]	General[3]	Total
National Park Service	649.6	231.4[4]	881.0
Forest Service	129.0	1,512.4[4]	1,641.4
Fish & Wildlife Service	95.2	290.1	385.3
Bureau of Land Management	17.6	2.8	20.8
	$891.4	$2,036.7	$2,928.1

Source: U.S. Department of the Interior, Heritage Recreation and Conservation Service, Division of Federal Lands Planning, 1981.

[1] After appropriations of amounts requested in Carter Budget for FY 1981. Amounts are based on lands to be acquired; not all inholdings are proposed for acquisition.

[2] For acquisition within areas specifically authorized by Congress.

[3] For acquisition of lands for L&WCF purposes under general authority as approved by the Land Policy Group, an advisory committee of the Assistant Secretary of the Interior for Fish, Wildlife and Parks.

[4] Estimate by U.S. Forest Service. The figure approved by the Land Policy Group is $1.169 billion.

that the owner of *any* property condemned by any agency of the federal government may select public lands of equal value (in lieu of dollars) as compensation for the taking.

Senator Harrison H. Schmitt (R-New Mexico) has proposed (S. 254) an extension of the White Sands bill to all public land states, authorizing them to select public lands in exchange for state lands in military reservations.

Congressman Philip M. Crane (R-Illinois) introduced a modern version of the Homestead Act (H.R. 2951) which would require the Secretary of the Interior to convey for a token fee not more than 160 acres to any person who applies for the land and within three years builds and occupies a house on it.

The significance of these bills overall is the sponsors' shared preference for bypassing key provisions of FLPMA. In each case, the Secretary of the Interior would be deprived of the discretion to decide that certain tracts would not be made available for selection. His discretion in the exchange bills is limited to establishing that the selected and offered lands are of approximately equal value. In the case of Mr. Crane's bill, lands could not be selected in national parks, forests, wildlife refuges, or wild and scenic rivers; outside those units, the only constraint on selection would be a prior selection under the same legislation.

The reasons for bypassing FLPMA in bills requiring public land exchanges for state inholdings in military reservations and for compensation to owners of lands acquired by the federal government through condemnation are obvious: to avoid secretarial discretion and also to circumvent the determinations of public and national interest and the requirements for land-use planning and public participation provided in the act. The same reasons, plus avoidance of the FLPMA fair-market-value requirement, apply to Congressman Crane's modern "Homestead Act."

The Utah Proposal

Unless Congress should respond to proposals for large-scale public sales to bolster the treasury, the greatest potential for major transfers of public land lies not in outright disposal, but in exchanges. Work is under way in several states on exchanges of various sizes. One state, Utah, has addressed the exchange issue with considerable vigor and proposed a decision process again outside the framework of FLPMA.

Governor Scott Matheson of Utah and Secretary Watt have agreed to work together on a proposal to "'block-up' state-owned lands in Utah through a comprehensive exchange with the Department of the Interior," as Governor Matheson described the objective in a letter of March 19, 1981, to Secretary Watt. The endeavor is described as a "model for other public land states." The Secretary warmly praised the approach and promised BLM's cooperation in a reply drafted on March 27, 1981. While the Utah procedures would involve informal cooperation with the Bureau of Land Management, the initiative in selection of lands to be exchanged is assumed to rest with state officials, and public hearings are to be held by the state, not by BLM.

The Utah exchange proposal does not involve the land-use planning and public participation processes provided for in FLPMA. Action on the exchange package is to be sought directly from Congress, without formal decisions, findings, or recommendations made by federal officials pursuant to FLPMA. The question of value—emphasized at several points in FLPMA—is described as "secondary." The governor's March 19 letter states: "Our responsibility is to provide the Congress with a rationale for the final package, not an accounting of dollars or acres." The letter adds: "If we proceed as though this is a business as usual exchange on a massive scale, the project is doomed."

In short, an assumption underlying the Utah exchange proposal seems to be that FLPMA is not an appropriate vehicle for effecting land exchange and disposal in Utah; instead, it is considered a barrier. Governor Matheson does not state this position directly,[3] but fears of the costs, complexity, and time requirements of "business as usual" land-use planning, and particularly value-determination processes, are implied in the March 19 letter and expanded upon in subsequent statements.

THE NEED FOR A RESPONSIBLE PUBLIC LAND TRANSFER PROGRAM

The current scene witnesses a procession of nonfederal interests seeking transfers of public lands. The federal government is characteristically in a defensive position—defensive because advocates of specific transfers know what they want and pursue their objectives with understandable vigor, and defensive because the government itself has not systematically identified the public lands that are most appropriate for federal retention and multiple-use management.

The need for the federal government to assess and decide the future of its public lands has been recognized at least since 1964, when the Classification and Multiple Use Act of 1964 (CMU) authorized the Bureau of Land Mangement to classify public lands as suitable for either retention or disposal. Charles H. Stoddard, then director of BLM, had urged the classification legislation. "The central goal," Stoddard wrote in 1966,

> was to classify lands susceptible to multiple resource use management and to identify those more proper for disposition and to obtain legislation to secure this objective. Defined boundaries, a name comparable to National Parks and Forests, colors on maps, signs at entrances and exits, etc., would finally give the public lands to be retained an identity not heretofore attained.

BLM worked on classification until 1969, categorizing 131 million acres as suitable for retention and 3 million acres for disposal. About 38 million acres had not been finally classified when the authority expired.[4] (See Table 4.)

In FLPMA, Congress ignored the earlier classifications and Stoddard's recommendations. The act asserted the general retention policy without attempting to establish the national interest in retention of specified public land areas, as had been the case in deliberate federal decisions establishing national parks, forests, and wildlife refuges. Most critically, FLPMA did not distinguish between more solidly blocked, and therefore more "manageable" areas, and the checkerboarded and scattered tracts where there are often problems of access or conflicting management objectives. Instead, FLPMA relied on the land-use planning process to implement the general retention policy for a diverse public land system that faces insistent pressure for disposal and exchange. The process, carried out with the cooperation of other landowners and managers and with the participation of affected interests, is to determine the potential effect of exchanges and disposal on the value and manageability of both public lands and related private, state, and other federal lands.

Unfortunately, demand for transfers has outstripped the pace of BLM's land-use planning. Relatively few resource areas even have approved land-use plans. Further, BLM land-use plans are to be revised at 6-to-10-year intervals, too infrequently to be responsive, in some cases, to urgent needs for exchange or disposal. Additionally, BLM plans are prepared using "resource area" boundaries (a resource area is the smallest BLM management unit) and thus do not, for an individual state, provide a sufficiently broad overview to support carefully reasoned responses to proposed large-scale state exchanges on the Utah model.

At present, the Bureau of Land Management is being pressed by the Administration for hasty action on transfers without deliberate and open consideration under FLPMA of the effects of these actions on the integrity and manageability of the remaining public land estate; on the communities and individuals dependent on these lands for livelihood, recreation, and other uses; on the national interest in the resource values involved; or on the distribution of revenues from leasing and development of public land resources.[5]

If responses are made to nonfederal initiatives before the lands most suitable for retention and management are identified through

TABLE 4

SELECTED DATA FROM PRIOR PUBLIC LAND CLASSIFICATION EFFORTS OF BUREAU OF LAND MANAGEMENT
(ACRES)

State	Public Land Acreage[1]	"Best Blocked Public Land Areas"[2]	Classified For Retention[3]	"Transfer Areas"[4]	Classified For Disposal[3]	Unclassified[5]
Arizona	12,750,681	11,450,000	10,159,114	720,000	707,908	1,510,298
California	15,192,489[6]	15,837,000[6]	12,120,194	2,257,000	94,568	1,418,839
Colorado	8,405,721	6,885,000	6,256,332	324,000	105,649	1,737,312
Idaho	12,059,257	9,820,000	5,740,846	875,000	172,466	2,709,366
Montana	6,324,495	5,201,000	5,106,362	933,000	164,756	1,120,408
Nevada	48,063,798	45,190,000	37,652,923	1,870,000	293,227	1,891,949
New Mexico	13,036,237	10,110,000	10,228,824	2,840,000	945,074	1,749,306
Oregon	15,586,982	14,827,000	13,055,239	492,000	171,105	2,092,719
Utah	22,973,519	22,400,000	18,070,037	530,000	208,620	2,234,187
Wyoming	17,454,822	14,630,000	12,447,974	635,000	63,805	4,879,092
TOTALS	171,848,001	156,350,000	130,837,845	11,476,000	2,927,178	21,343,476[7]

[1] From U.S. Department of Interior, Bureau of Land Management, *Public Land Statistics, 1969,* (Washington D.C.: Government Printing Office, 1970).

[2] From "Initial Analysis" of potential land classifications prepared in-house by BLM in response to Udall memorandum of December, 1963. Table dated October, 1964.

[3] From U.S. Department of the Interior, Bureau of Land Management, "Public Land Classification Progress," a report on actions by BLM under the Classification and Use Act, September 1, 1970.

[4] From "Initial Analysis" dated October, 1964. Assumed to be suitable for disposal; consisted largely of scattered tracts; did not include checkerboard areas (private communication, BLM staff).

[5] From "Public Land Classification Progress."

[6] The discrepancy (a larger acreage of "best blocked" areas than total public land acreage) probably arises from completed surveys in California of previously unsurveyed lands between the 1964 delineation of "best blocked" areas and the data of compilation of the 1969 Public Land Statistics.

[7] An incomplete figure. Actually, no final classification action was taken on approximately 38.7 million acres. The Bureau had proposed 147.6 million acres to be classified for retention and multiple use management. Only 130.85 million acres were so classified. Apparently no final classification action was ever taken on the remaining 16.7 million acres before the CMU authority expired in 1969. The 22 million acres shown in this column never formally received a proposed classification.

processes established in FLPMA, the remaining public land estate could be substantially compromised. Even more fragmentation would follow. Existing uses would be disrupted, administration and assembly of economic units for resource production would be more difficult, and opportunities for protection of aesthetic values and ecologically significant systems might be lost.

Two Administration initiatives are particularly troublesome—the White House program to sell off unspecified portions of the public lands as "surplus" property to produce income for the Treasury, and Secretary Watt's earlier proposal to use public land exchanges to compensate owners of private lands acquired by the government in national parks, wildlife refuges, wilderness areas, forests, and wild and scenic rivers.[6]

What is most certain about these proposals is that individual selections of desirable public land tracts would be based on self-interest, not the "public interest" or "national interest" prescribed by FLPMA as tests for exchanges and sales, respectively.

Inevitably, a wholesale invitation to comb the public lands for private acquisitions would generate a high percentage of selections deliberately made to secure leverage over use of surrounding lands. A relatively small acquisition, for instance, could permit an owner to control access to large land areas otherwise attractive and available for public outdoor recreation purposes. Acquisitions of small tracts within relatively solid blocks of public wildland areas could, intentionally or unintentionally, substantially impair prospects of wilderness designation. In mineralized areas, private parties could acquire small tracts important for access to or logical development of mining operations, complicating assembly of economic units.

The prospect of "high-grading" the public lands through Administration-fostered private sales and exchanges would also interfere—perhaps critically—with the prospect of "blocking up" state and federal ownerships in the West, including major initiatives for that purpose as proposed by Governor Matheson and by this paper.

A Proposal for a Public Land Transfer Program Based on FLPMA

The federal government can be helpful in facilitating sensible public/private exchanges by being genuinely forthcoming in identifying public lands available for such purposes, by being equally clear about lands that will not be available, and by responding promptly to bona fide expressions of interest. FLPMA provides basic authority and processes for a responsible exchange and disposal program that incorporates these goals. It calls for:

• National interest and public interest tests for disposal and exchange, including, in the case of exchanges, requirements for explicit consideration of better federal land management, needs of state and local people, the economy, community expansion, and the full range of resource values.

• A land-use planning process open to all affected interests, with special requirements for public participation, consideration of neighboring landowners, and consistency with state and local plans.

• Requirements for equal value in exchanges and for fair market value in disposal (with exceptions).

• Discretion for the Secretary of the Interior on exchange and disposal actions.

The Federal Land Policy and Management Act should be the basis of an aggressive program to address currently heated issues of public land retention, disposal, and management policy in the West. What is missing from FLPMA—or more precisely what is missing in carrying out FLPMA—is a deliberate effort to assess and act on land tenure adjustments in ways that anticipate changing needs in a growing West. This could be provided either by the Congress or the Secretary of the Interior in the form of a deliberate program, operating within the policies and processes set forth in FLPMA, to identify those lands that should remain in federal multiple-use management, to evaluate and facilitate large-scale exchanges where ownership patterns suggest the need, and to identify those public lands that might best be offered for disposal, either as trading stock for consolidation of existing federal areas or through outright disposal.

This paper proposes a revision and updating of the previous classification of public lands for retention/disposal performed under the Classification and Multiple Use Act of 1964, modified to include large-scale exchanges, and using FLPMA authorities, mandates, and processes. Rather than being a barrier to effective and efficient decision making about public lands, FLPMA establishes the processes and guidelines for achieving optimum economic and environmental values on the public lands and, to a lesser extent, state and private lands.

The program proposed here, to be carried out by the Bureau of Land Management following widespread consultations on program policy, procedure, and criteria, should be designed as a two-year planning effort. This time frame is more than adequate, given the westwide wilderness inventory of the public lands completed in 1980, prior land-use planning, and recent work on potential exchanges and on identification of public lands needed for state and local community expansion and public purposes. The planning period would be followed by aggressive implementation in accordance with findings of the planning program. The objectives are:

• To identify (and to amend land-use plans to delineate) those public land areas which, by reason of resource values, uses, and configuration of ownership, are most important and most suitable for retention and purposeful management by the federal government under the FLPMA general retention policy.

• To identify and evaluate against FLPMA criteria potential large-scale exchanges with states and with major private landholders in checkerboard areas, where warranted;[7] and to amend land-use plans to provide for appropriate exchanges, subject to refinement based on more detailed examination of the resources and values involved—again in the context of FLPMA criteria.

• To identify those public lands suitable for disposal, with priority given to (1) meeting community expansion needs, and state and community needs under the Recreation and Public Purpose Act; (2) using such lands as trading stock for consolidation of ownership in existing federal areas (including exchanges to block up ownerships in public land retention areas); (3) assisting in needed acquisition in national parks and wildlife refuges; and (4) offering such lands to private parties at fair market value.[8]

• To take timely action to implement planning decisions in prime retention areas, and to carry out exchanges and sales determined to meet FLPMA public interest and national interest tests.

The process should take place in formal cooperation with governors and state land commissions and should involve widespread public participation.[9] Special efforts may be necessary to secure the cooperation of local governments.

There should be no general moratorium on public land transfers during the planning period. Satisfaction of state in-lieu selections should proceed on current schedules; the planning base for this work is well advanced in several states. Routine transactions should continue to the extent manpower is available, with priority given to responding to community expansion and public purpose needs of local and state governments.

Programs to offer public lands for private exchanges or for sale— whether to cut federal budget deficits or to compensate owners of nonfederal lands acquired in other land systems—should await completion of the program, and should then be confined to lands found suitable for these purposes through the planning process. Interest in private sales and exchanges should be solicited and evaluated against FLPMA criteria during the planning period.

No large-scale transfers such as the proposed Utah exchange should be consummated, either by the Congress or by executive branch officials, until the FLPMA-based planning process has been completed for the public lands involved. As planning is completed, approved exchanges and sale offerings should be pursued vigorously. The pace of actual transfers will be determined by availability of manpower for various kinds of work involved in realty transactions. Money and positions for the BLM lands and realty staff will be the key.

The BLM wilderness review process presents some complications. About 24 million acres of public lands have been identified by BLM as potential additions to national wilderness areas. The integrity of these lands must be protected until Congress decides whether they are to be designated as wilderness or not. This necessary waiting period will delay some potential exchanges.

The magnitude of economic and environmental values involved, and the potential effects of large-scale transfers on communities, users of all kinds, and distribution of revenues from public land development all suggest the need for a special effort to shape the program in consultation with elected officials from every section of the United States (with some special care for the views of western states and communities), and with bona fide representatives of all who are interested in how public lands are managed.

These consultation processes are particularly critical in view of the concerns of many conservation organizations and interests about the Administration's environmental commitment, and perceptions of political leaders in other sections of the country—such as the Council of Northeastern Governors (CONEG)—of a pro-western bias in Administration domestic policies generally.

A logical way to begin an intensive consultation process would be for the Administration to formulate a reasonably detailed draft program statement that would include:

• A statement of problems, opportunities, and objectives.
• Acknowledgment of relevant FLPMA provisions.
• A date for completion of the planning phase, and a target date or dates and schedules for accomplishing actual transfers.
• Procedures for carrying out the program.
• Criteria for "classifying" lands and evaluating transactions—both fully consistent with FLPMA.
• Money and manpower commitments.

The consultation process might well include hearings by the Senate Energy and Natural Resources Committee and the House Interior and Insular Affairs Committee. Following consultation, a revised program statement should be offered for additional comment; any final document and subsequent guidance to the field should reflect the assurance of "fairness," access, and conformity to existing law demanded by the gravity of the decisions to be made.

A public national commitment should help assure responsiveness by BLM field staff in making suitable lands available for disposal. Such a commitment also would assure governors and western state land agencies that the Administration is going to sustain the effort and produce results. Detailed guidance to ensure uniformity in methods (but preferably not results) should be issued by BLM's Washington office, and should also be subject to public review.

Early consultation by the state directors of BLM with governors and other state officials will be necessary to establish firm cooperative relationships, including state commitments to cooperative efforts on exchanges. In fact, it would probably not be prudent to make any serious inquiry into large-scale exchanges with states unless firm agreements can be reached with key state officials before the program is initiated.

While local as well as state viewpoints warrant careful consideration, final decisions on actual exchanges to be implemented on the basis of land-use plans should be made by the BLM state director in order to assure a statewide perspective.

Exchange and disposal actions following completion of classification could be taken by authorized officers of BLM under existing law and delegations. Director or Secretarial approval might be wise for transactions beyond a certain scale in acres or dollar values, and consultations with Congress on large-scale transactions might be appropriate, even where not required by law.[10] The pace of actual transfers will depend on the procedures adopted and on the availability of manpower and money for professional staff and services (as well as an agreement between exchanging parties). A later section of this paper discusses some ways in which procedure and resolution of value questions could be facilitated.

Action is also needed to confirm the boundaries of the areas found to be suitable for retention and long-term, multiple-use management. This should, at a minimum, be reflected in mapping and boundary-marking programs of state and district BLM offices. Congressional approval of these areas as "national resource land areas" or some other designation may be appropriate in order to provide a dependable basis for planning, budgeting, and on-the-ground management. This designation should be reflected in appropriate allocations of money and manpower by the Congress and the Bureau.

The program proposed here has a number of advantages:

• It confirms the federal government's intent to seek more sensible ownership patterns for land in the West.

• It provides access for all affected interests to a decision process based on existing law, and includes land-use planning, Secretarial discretion, and equal-value and fair-market-value concepts, all of which are critical to sustained public support and the best defense against fears or allegations of "giveaway."

• It would lead to clear demarcation of those portions of the public lands found to be suitable for long-term, multiple-use management under FLPMA.

• It reconfirms the federal government's intent to satisfy quickly a state's entitlement to in-lieu lands, and to respond to needs of state and local governments for lands for community expansion and public purposes.

• It can be presented in the form of a program document to key congressional committees, governors, and others for comment, refinement, and endorsement.

• It will make possible significant transfers within no more than two or three years, and provide a base of both information and recorded public preference that will support future land tenure adjustments.

The approach also involves some disadvantages:

• It may be seen as an over-elaborate exercise likely to slow down rather than accelerate transfers. Some may question the commitment of the current Administration to environmental values and to national interest considerations.

• Manpower costs will be substantial.

• From the standpoint of those wishing to acquire public land, it will constrain freedom of selection by identifying areas to be retained permanently by the federal government; formal public participation, equal-value and fair-market-value concepts, and determinations of national and public interests may also be seen as constraints.

Given current controversy over ownership and management policies for public lands, the prospect of gaining and sustaining public confidence in a large-scale program for land transfers will ultimately depend on whether the program is perceived as fair and equitable. A program conducted under explicit and generally accepted procedures should result in a more productive and more judicious transfer program than a series of *ad hoc* proposals subject to characterization as "deals" and open to political attack and judicial challenge.

The process recommended here is neither obscure nor unfamiliar. The Bureau of Land Management and a reasonable array of constituencies will remember the classification process under the 1964 Classification and Multiple Use Act. Both the RARE II wilderness review of the national forests and the inventory of public lands throughout the West for wilderness suitability, conducted by BLM from 1978 to 1980, were similar. In short, state and local governments and public land constituents of all kinds know how to play the game.

Some Questions To Be Considered

The argument made in this paper—that FLPMA can be used as the basis of a responsible transfer program—does not assume perfection in current policy and practice. Two major questions to be addressed are whether FLPMA should be amended, and how the problem of value should be dealt with.

SHOULD FLPMA BE AMENDED?

Certain features of FLPMA seem essential to public confidence in a responsible transfer program. These include: the general retention policy; the land-use planning process as a way of securing public participation in making exchange and disposal decisions; equal value in exchange; fair market value for disposal; and discretion for the Secretary of the Interior (and those exercising his delegated authority) in deciding whether specific tracts will be available for exchange or disposal as determined through the land-use planning process and national interest and public interest tests.

Other features are problematic. For instance, FLPMA provides that either party to an exchange involving public lands may pay up to 25 percent in cash to achieve equal value, a provision designed to ease the "closing" of exchange transactions by not requiring precise equalization in land values. There is probably not enough history to evaluate this provision definitively. The cash-equalization feature may prove more useful to private parties than to federal or state interests. Whether 25 percent is the "right" figure is uncertain.

Some observers see as a problem FLPMA's provision that public lands may be exchanged only for lands within the same state.

While this has been the case in specific circumstances, as a general rule, this provision may facilitate rather than limit exchanges. This is principally because both states and local governments receive revenues from public lands: states receive a portion of the receipts from lease of minerals and other commodities; local governments receive payments in lieu of taxes. Understandably, states and local governments frequently are opposed to exchanges and sales that would reduce revenues, and thus are more likely to accept exchanges within governmental units. Moreover, if a bold program of consolidating state and federal ownership is undertaken, an out-of-state exchange may be seen as competitive with both state and federal ambitions to "block up."

More compelling reasons for amendment of FLPMA would be to secure specific congressional endorsement for an aggressive program (while confirming the policies of general retention, land-use planning, intergovernmental cooperation, equal value and fair market value, and Secretarial discretion); to provide an opportunity for congressional review of exchanges beyond a certain scale; to provide congressional confirmation of the integrity of those public land areas found to be most appropriate for long-term federal management under FLPMA (consistent with Stoddard's recommendations, noted earlier); and to earmark a portion of receipts from public land sales to supplement Land and Water Conservation Fund appropriations for previously authorized federal land acquisition.

THE QUESTION OF VALUE

The most difficult problem in a significant transfer program may well prove to be value. This paper has argued that concepts of equal value and fair market value must be applied to transfers of public land, both out of "fairness" to all affected interests and to sustain public support for transactions involving immense monetary and other values.

Problems may arise from a number of quarters: from failure on the part of potential exchanging parties to recognize the concepts of equal value and fair market value as appropriate "rules of the game" for transfers (large-scale, state-federal exchanges are particularly vulnerable to politically generated expectations that one side or the other ought to emerge with a clear advantage from "equal-value" exchanges); from differences of opinion (and professional appraisers' findings) over valuations of specific tracts; from differences over valuation methodologies, particularly where large acreages are involved; and from the costs and time of value-determination processes.

Solutions to technical issues in value determination are beyond the scope of this paper. It is assumed that realty and mineral-resource appraisal experts in and out of government are working on such perennial problems as finding ways to "arbitrate" disparate appraisals and to reduce the costs of determining mineral values.[11] There are, however, some important questions appropriate for discussion here.

FLPMA's language on exchanges comes close to posing a central issue—whether fair market value as determined through standard appraisal practices should be the *only* measure used to determine equal value in an exchange. Section 206 (a) authorizes exchanges when the Secretary of the Interior finds they serve the public interest. Consideration is to be given to "better federal land management and needs of state and local people, including needs for lands for the economy, community expansion, recreation areas, food, fiber, and fish and wildlife"—a litany of the multiple-use values listed elsewhere in FLPMA, except minerals, wilderness, and cultural values. Further, the subsection provides that when considering an exchange, the "values *and objectives*" that public lands would serve if retained in federal ownership "should be . . . not more than the values of the nonfederal lands [to be acquired] . . . *and the public objectives* that would be served . . ." by those lands (emphasis added). Section 206 (b) provides that the values of lands exchanged "either shall be equal, or if they are not equal, the value shall be equalized by the payment of money" up to 25 percent of value—a clear requirement for standard appraisal practice as the sole determinant of value.

The Secretary of the Interior is thus enjoined to consider the broad question of better federal land management and sound land use, generally and in specific—but cannot approve an exchange based on these considerations unless the lands involved are of equal value as measured by accepted real-property appraisal practices.

Any resource manager, one would think, would be profesionally pleased at the prospect of optimizing the total mix of "values and objectives" that might be represented in a potential exchange. This prospect has been advanced in a limited context, in fact, by an assistant attorney general of the state of Utah[12] in a memorandum to Governor Matheson noting that "Special Value Exchanges" would involve "lands like the magnificent Jacob Hamlin Arch . . . located on state lands in the scenic Coyote Gulch area, and it would be as difficult to arrive at a dollar value of that arch as it would be to arrive at a dollar value of Rainbow Bridge."

Standing firm on current market value as the basis for evaluating exchanges does not, of course, preclude consideration of other public-interest criteria. And departing from market value poses a serious risk of both abuse and infinite variations in judgment about values not susceptible to precise measurement. Caution is appropriate.

The prospect is interesting enough, however, to ask whether methodologies that assess certain nonmarket values in other resource management fields might not be adaptable to land exchanges, at least to land exchanges with states. The "Principles and Standards" developed by the U.S. Water Resources Council for formulation, evaluation, and review of water resource projects are based in part on a generation or more of scholarly attempts to improve units of measure for recreation, fish and wildlife habitats, and other "nonmarket" values. A serious look at the "Principles and Standards" and related work in water resources and other fields might offer some improved guidance for both national interest determinations (in disposal) and public interest determinations (in exchange). One might even be able to formulate a dual evaluation system (a "public interest" account and a "fair market value" determination) and provide some flexibility beyond adjustments in acreage or cash equalization where "public interest" values are so clearly superior on one side of an exchange as to offset a disparity in market value.

Even without a formal dual system of measuring value, it can be predicted that something approaching a dual system will actually operate in expressions of public preference on federal-state exchanges. In large-scale exchanges in the western states, state governments characteristically operate through state land boards and commissions. These agencies are bound by law or constitution to maximize revenues for specific beneficiaries (the common schools, the university system, and so on) in management of lands. The states can be expected, generally, to put a premium on revenue-producing lands and resources in exchange negotiations. Environmentally concerned citizens and organizations, on the other hand, have historically tended to see the federal government as a more dependable protector of resource systems of particular environmental value or vulnerability. A public hearing record on state-federal exchanges in most western states will almost certainly support exchanges that would give state governments a more-than-equal "deal" on revenue-producing resources, with a corresponding bias toward federal retention of areas of special environmental value. Within reason, it may well be in the "public interest" to devise a way to respond to such expressions.

There are also complications in the accepted processes of value determination. And there may be some ways to make "precise" and costly determinations less important and less burdensome.

For lands not currently known or suspected to contain significant mineral values, it may be possible to justify exchanges based on surface values. Cost and time requirements are much more burdensome and significant in cases involving mineral resources. The U.S. Geological Survey (USGS), in effect, ranks public land areas from the standpoint of mineral characteristics ("prospectively valuable," "valuable," "known geologic structure," and so on). USGS also makes, or consults with BLM on, value determination on specific tracts.

The most troubling issue may arise when a state wants to secure lands known to contain rich mineral resources (for instance, Utah's persistent interest in oil-shale lands), and wishes to offer a much larger acreage of state lands in exchange. In such cases, the costs and time required to establish the values of offered lands may be burdensome indeed. In the absence of comparative sale information as a firm basis for establishing values, extensive drilling and discounted cash flow value methods may be called for, with consequent costs and infinite grist for argument.

The value question is important primarily because of state interest in acquiring mineral lands and because of the special problems of mineral value determination. The intensity of state interest in acquiring lands of high mineral values seems to reflect an assumption that state ownership would produce dramatic increases in income to the state.

The case is not so compelling as it appears at first glance. The western states now receive substantial sums from the public lands— nearly 50 percent of the receipts from oil, gas, coal, and other mineral leases (an estimated $1.36 billion for 1982); appropriated payments in lieu of taxes ($95.5 million in 1982, though the Administration proposes cutting this to $45 million for fiscal 1983); and additional sums ($451 million in 1982) for water development projects in the West.[13] Furthermore, the federal government bears the full cost of managing the lands; state receipts come "off the top," not from net federal revenues.

States might add more to their *net* benefits by concentrating on using state lands as trading stock for federal lands which may generate state revenues as sites for industrial, commercial, and residential development, as opposed to exchanging their current holdings for federal lands from which they already receive the lion's share of income. Arizona's Governor Bruce Babbitt has followed this strategy in selecting "in lieu" lands owed the state by the federal government. Such a federal strategy would also avoid the special problems of mineral valuation.

It may be useful for the executive branch (or the Congress) to contract with a qualified independent institution to study and make recommendations on refined systems for value determinations to support a large-scale program of land transfers. Perhaps the combination of a fresh perspective and newer technologies will produce methods that will permit reasonable valuation in all but the most difficult circumstances at bearable cost.

It is also conceivable that some novel arrangements in which the federal government and the state share revenues on exchanged lands for a specified period might make costly valuation processes less critical.

Epilogue: Is There a Constituency for a Rational Approach to the Public Land Transfer Issue?

This paper argues that the "best" way—and quite possibly the only way—to effect significant improvements in patterns of state, federal, and private landownership in the western United States is to design and carry out a visible and systematic program through policies and procedures specified by Congress in the Federal Land Policy and Management Act of 1976.

The case for a "rational" approach seems obvious. Yet, in a period of an outpouring of proposals for both exchange and outright disposition of portions of the public estate, none of the major parties at interest has proposed an approach based on existing law, normal principles, and procedures.

If the case for the rational approach is in the public interest, who—if anyone—is likely to emerge as its champion?

The Reagan Administration, in all candor, seems an unlikely prospect. The Secretary of the Interior has committed himself publicly to support of the Utah "Project Bold" approach, in which an individual state develops a package of state-federal exchanges and other transfer proposals, manages the process of securing public comment, and seeks congressional consent without federal officials having met their responsibilities under FLPMA. Further, the Administration is moving ahead with its plan to sell public lands—to what extent is not clear—to bolster the national treasury, apparently presuming that disposal is in the national interest despite FLPMA's general retention policy.

There also is the question of whether even a well-considered Administration initiative would inspire effective national support without a painful period of argument about policy, process, criteria, and anticipated results.

Many leaders of the nation's organized conservation community made clear at a meeting of the Natural Resources Council of America in November 1981 that they would demand extraordinary assurances that national and environmental interests and values would be effectively protected before they could support a major program under an Administration they believe to be biased toward the interests of resource-using industries.

Political leaders of other regions of the country—already smarting under what they describe as pro-western, pro-Sun Belt tilts in domestic policy—may not assume that the interests of their regions will be seriously reflected in a program which may involve the transfer of federal energy and mineral resources to states in the Sunbelt and the energy-rich mountain "OPEC" states.

LEADERSHIP NEEDED

The situation may require leadership of a high order from the Congress and from the western governors as well as the Administration if we are to achieve significant improvements in land-ownership patterns in the West.

Governor Matheson of Utah is in a position of both special difficulty and special opportunity. His "Project Bold" is the first comprehensive statewide effort to rationalize state and public land patterns. The state is entering a second round of hearings on potential transfers, and reportedly does not anticipate federal action before 1983. However, legislation ratifying a proposal developed by and presumably favoring the interests of the state of Utah is not, in my judgment, likely to survive attacks from those concerned with national and regional equities, environmental values, and general public interest concepts.

It also seems possible that controversy over the Utah approach may endanger the prospect of widespread public support for land tenure adjustments in other states, in the form either of similar state-by-state legislative packages or a westwide FLPMA-based program.

In these circumstances, the interests of Utah and other western states, and the nation, might well be served by a recommendation from the Governor of Utah that the Bureau of Land Management complete as quickly as possible a statewide land-use planning and public involvement process under FLPMA to consider Utah-BLM transactions in the FLPMA context, and to seek implementing action under FLPMA rather than a Congressional bypass of FLPMA. Given the amount of analysis already done by the state (with substantial informal participation by BLM staff), a responsible analysis under FLPMA should be possible in a year or less.

The outcome of an exchange program in Utah, one assumes, would be somewhat different as a result of FLPMA's equal value concepts, and increased leverage for national and environmental interests participating in the planning process. The record of public preference undoubtedly will reflect the primary interest of the state in securing revenue-producing lands; it will probably also reveal a preference for federal administration of environmentally sensitive areas: no windfalls, perhaps, for any interest, but a legacy of more effective land use and management.

Most of the western governors, in private communications with the author, have taken a wait-and-see stance on the Utah model, in part a reflection of the immense regard in which Governor Matheson is held. His leadership in proposing an assessment and decision process based on FLPMA as a more dependable basis for adjusting landownerhsip patterns in *all* the western states might (and, one hopes, would) lead to the endorsement by the Western Governors' Conference of a formal cooperative program along the lines I have outlined.

Given the number of current transfer proposals and the values involved, it is time for the Congress to assert itself. The vigorous exercise of oversight responsibilities by the House Interior and Insular Affairs Committee and the Senate Energy and Natural Resources Committee could help assess the consistency of current Administration policies and actions on land transfers with law, legislative intent, and various perspectives of the public interest. Oversight hearings would provide a forum for exposure and debate on bills now before the Congress, on evolving public land sale proposals, and on the implications of Project Bold. Oversight hearings could also provide the vehicle for bargaining among political leaders from all regions, the range of resource use and environmental/recreational interests, the Congress, and the Administration about how best to approach the problems of landownership patterns in the West.

The ''rational'' approach to the problem needs a constituency. That constituency can be built on leadership from the western governors and the Congress (with the Administration cooperating, if not leading), around the theme of a responsible program fashioned and carried out with the participation of all interests.

The alternative is most likely to be a protracted period of controversy and posturing, in which assigning blame for failure to achieve more sensible land patterns will have to substitute for the satisfaction of responsible action.

References

1. "The policy of large-scale disposal of public lands . . . should be revised and . . . future disposal should be of only those lands that will achieve maximum benefit for the general public in non-Federal ownership. . . ." Public Land Law Review Commission, *One Third of the Nation's Land: A Report to the President and to the Congress by the Public Land Law Review Commission* (Washington, D.C.: Government Printing Office, 1970).

2. "Questions and Answers, Disposal of Federal Property," Fact Sheet distributed by Bureau of Land Management, dated February 11, 1982.

3. The Utah proposal asserts certain "entitlements" to public lands that have not been recognized by the federal government. If these were to be recognized administratively as a basis for transfer of public lands, it seems likely that court challenges would follow. The decision by Utah to seek direct congressional approval of a transfer package may be based, in part, on this problem.

4. An earlier review performed by BLM in response to instructions from Secretary of the Interior Stewart L. Udall in December 1963 had identified 11.5 million acres as suitable for disposal.

5. The amounts and distribution of monies paid by industry for use of public land resources is likely to be a significant factor in assessing transfer proposals. For FY 1982, public land receipts are estimated by BLM at $1.36 billion. The total may be expected to increase substantially as over-thrust belt oil and gas wells on federal lands go into production and coal and geothermal production rises in response to efforts to reduce dependence on foreign oil. Under current laws apportioning receipts, about one-third accrues to the federal treasury. The balance returns to the West—in the form of direct payments and in support for western water projects through earmarking to the Reclamation Fund.

6. The issue is not new. Charles F. Wheatley, *et al.*, discussed the conflict in *Study of Land Acquisitions and Exchanges Related to Retention and Management or Disposition of Federal Public Lands*, a report prepared for the Public Land Law Review Commission, 1970 (Springfield, Va.: National Technical Information Service, 1970). Basically, Wheatley concluded that the final "classification" authority should continue to rest with BLM as being "in more of an impartial position to judge the merits of releasing the selected public lands to nonfederal ownership, than would the Park Service." The Wheatley report is distinguished by a number of case histories recording successes and failures in land exchanges, and is useful reading in the present context of exchange and disposal generally, beyond the parks/public lands issue.

7. This paper does not assume that formal efforts will be made to resolve the checkerboard issue in each case. A three-way cooperative agreement involving BLM, the state, and the principal private landowner in the checkerboard would appear to be necessary to sustain any hope of action on a large scale. An alternative (not discussed in this paper) might be to amend FLPMA to permit some special cooperative management arrangements on checkerboard areas.

8. While not addressed in this paper, serious consideration should be given to congressional earmarking of receipts from public land sales to help support needed federal acquisitions—arguably, a far more dependable way of facilitating urgently needed acquisitions in national conservation system units than exchanges would be. In time and money, exchanges are far more costly to administer than sales as a consequence of doubling appraisal and realty work and negotiations over tract selections.

9. In private communications, Stoddard and others have said that there was significant local resistance to disposal classifications during the Classification and Multiple Use Act effort. In a 1963 in-house classification effort based on land-use patterns, BLM personnel identified 11.5 million acres as suitable for disposal. Several years later under CMU, BLM classified only 3 million acres for disposal (although another 38 million acres were never classified either for retention or disposal). The difference in disposal acreage in these two efforts might be that there was extensive public involvement in the CMU process. At public hearings on classification proposals, public land users, including livestock permittees and timber operators, spoke in significant numbers against disposal of even scattered and nominally unmanageable tracts. One may assume that many economic users enjoy—or believe that they enjoy—benefits that might be lost in public land disposal or exchange.

10. Congress now has the prerogative of reviewing sales above 2,500 acres and administrative actions that would prohibit one or more multiple uses on tracts of over 100,000 acres.

11. The U.S. Geological Survey, as reported in personal conversations, has been working on this subject for several months through its Conservation Division. The Senate Energy and Natural Resources Committee sponsored a workshop in July 1981 which generated suggestions on appraisal practices.

12. Richard L. Dewsnip, Assistant Attorney General of Utah, to Governor Scott M. Matheson, "Suggested Structure for Bold Program," memorandum of February 18, 1981.

13. Telephone interview with Robert P. Henry, Bureau of Land Management, February 17, 1982.